The Hanukkah Story

First published in 2004 by Evans Brothers Ltd.
2A Portman Mansions, Chiltern Street, London W1U 6NR

Text copyright © 2004 Anita Ganeri
Illustrations copyright © 2004 Evans Brothers Ltd.

The text of *The Hanukkah Story* is based on *Judah Saves the Jews*, one of nine stories first published in *Jewish Stories*, a title in the *Storyteller* series published by Evans Brothers Ltd.

Editor: Louise John
Designer: Robert Walster
Illustrations: Rachael Phillips, Allied Artists
Production: Jenny Mulvanny
Consultant: Jonathan Gorsky

Published in the United States by Smart Apple Media
1980 Lookout Drive, North Mankato, Minnesota 56003

Library of Congress Cataloging–in–Publication Data

Ganeri, Anita, 1961–
The Hanukkah story / Anita Ganeri ; illustrated by Rachael Phillips.
p. cm. — (Holiday stories)
ISBN 1-58340-490-2
1. Hanukkah—Juvenile literature. [1. Hanukkah. 2. Holidays.] I. Phillips, Rachael, ill. II. Title. III. Series.

BM695.H3G35 2004
296.4'35—dc22   2003067292

9 8 7 6 5 4 3 2 1

Acknowledgments:
For permission to reproduce copyright material, the author and publishers gratefully acknowledge the following:
page 20 Trip
page 21 Trip

The Hanukkah Story

Anita Ganeri

Illustrated by
Rachael Phillips

A⁺

Contents

More than 2,000 years ago, a Greek king named Antiochus ruled over a vast empire. In every land of his empire, he ordered people to give up their own religious beliefs and worship the Greek gods instead. Only the Jews in Israel refused to obey the king.

"Blessed is he that comes in the name of the Lord," they shouted. "Hosanna in the highest."

The Jews wanted to follow their own religion. They wanted to worship one God and no other, as they had been taught in their holy books. But King Antiochus wanted the Jews to follow Greek customs and traditions. Furious, he decided to punish the Jews and destroy the Jewish religion.

King Antiochus stopped the Jews from following the teaching of the Torah, their holy book. He forbade them from keeping their holy day of rest and prayer, the Shabbat, sacred. Then he sent his soldiers to the holy city of Jerusalem. They ransacked the Temple—the Jews' most sacred place—where they worshiped God. The soldiers stole the Temple treasures and snuffed out the special oil lamp that burned day and night as a symbol of God's presence.

A statue of the Greek god Zeus was set up in the Temple. Antiochus ordered that every Jew must sacrifice a pig to Zeus. This was a cruel thing to ask, because according to Jewish law, pigs were considered unclean. Anyone who refused to obey was killed.

Even though their lives were in danger, many Jews refused to obey the king's command. But how could they fight against the Greeks when their numbers were so small?

Not far away from Jerusalem, in the small town of Modi'in, there lived an old priest named Mattathias and his five sons. Mattathias and his sons refused to make a sacrifice to the Greek gods. They pulled down statues of Greek gods in the town, killed the soldier who read out the king's orders, and fled to the nearby hills to hide. Soon, more and more Jews joined them. They wanted to stay true to God, and they were ready to risk their lives for Him.

When Mattathias died, one of his sons, Judah, took over command. He organized the Jews into an army to fight for freedom. When King Antiochus saw what was going on, he was furious. Determined to crush the Jews once and for all, he gathered a mighty army and led them into battle against the Jews.

As the two sides lined up to fight, the small band of Jews were dismayed to see how big the Greek army was. What chance did they stand against such a great force? But Judah would not let his men become discouraged.

"The king's army is large," he told them. "But we are fighting for God. He will protect us."

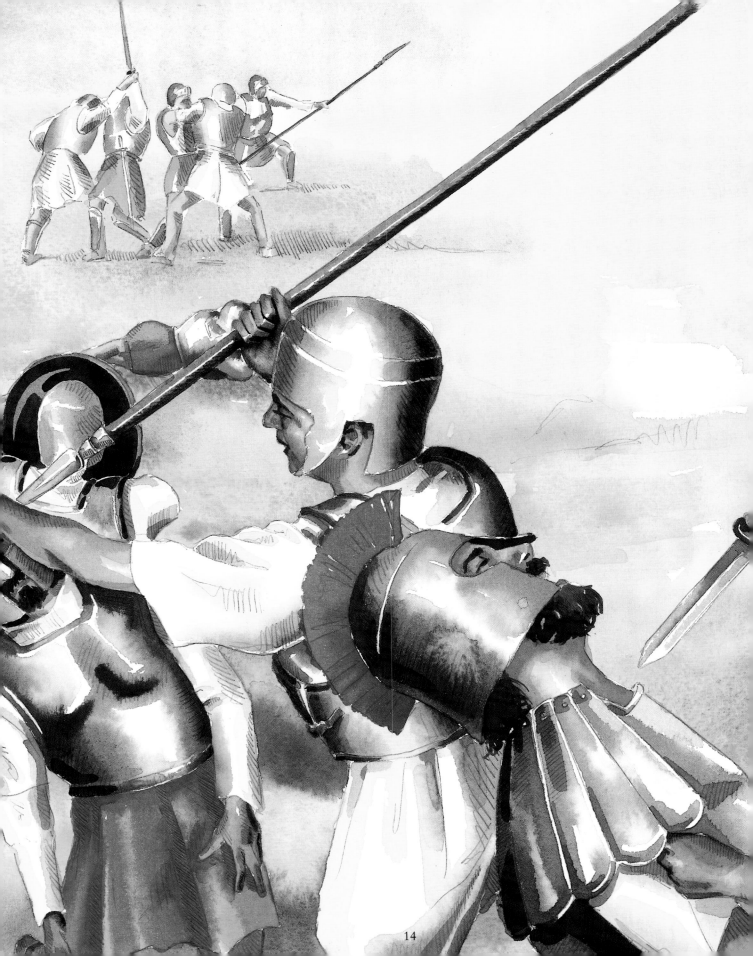

In the battle that followed, Judah's army was brave and fought hard against the Greeks. Even though they were greatly outnumbered, the Jews won a great victory. It seemed that God was truly on their side, watching over them. Many more victories followed against Antiochus's forces. In time, the little army of Jews drove the enemy out of Jerusalem.

Triumphantly, Judah led the Jews into their holy city. They flocked to the Temple to thank God for their victory, but a dreadful sight met their eyes.

"The first thing we must do," said Judah, "is repair all of the damage to our sacred Temple."

The Jews took down the images of the Greek gods. Then they began cleaning the Temple and making it holy.

When they were finished, Judah said, "We must light the oil lamp's flame again to celebrate our victory. Then the Temple will belong to God once more."

But when the Jews looked for oil to light the lamp, they saw that every jar of oil in the Temple had been broken. Suddenly, Judah spotted a jar hidden in a corner, but it was almost empty. There was just enough oil to keep the lamp burning for one day. It would take eight days for Judah's men to get more. What was Judah to do?

Judah lit the lamp. To his amazement, it did not go out at the end of the day. Instead, it kept burning the next day, and the next, and the day after that. In fact, it kept burning for eight whole days, long enough for the Jews to get fresh supplies of oil. A great miracle had happened.

Since that time, Jewish people have celebrated the festival of Hanukkah. They light lamps to remember the miracle that happened in the Temple long ago. They remember how God showed them that He was always with them and how they won the freedom to worship Him.

The Hanukkah Lamp

During the festival of Hanukkah, Jews look back at this special time in their history and remember God's great miracle. They light eight candles on a special candlestick: one on the first night of Hanukkah, two on the second, and so on until all eight are lit. The ninth candle, in the center, is used

for lighting the others. (In the time of Judah, the Hanukkah candlestick had only seven candles, not nine.) Before lighting each candle, special prayers and blessings are said. Hanukkah, the festival of lights, usually takes place in December.

The Meaning of Hanukkah

The story of Hanukkah is about people sticking to their own beliefs and values, even when this puts their lives in danger. The Jews did not want to be forced to give up God's commandments or stop being themselves. The story teaches that being different is not easy, but sometimes it is more important to stand up for what you believe than to accept what you do not believe.

A Hanukkah Recipe

At Hanukkah, people eat food fried in oil to remember the miracle of the oil in the Temple lamp. Have an adult help you make your own tasty potato latkes (pancakes) for Hanukkah.

Ingredients:

6 medium potatoes
1 medium onion
2 eggs
2 tablespoons plain flour
1 teaspoon baking powder
salt and pepper
oil for frying

What to do:

1. Peel and grate the potatoes. Squeeze as much water out of them as possible.
2. Beat the eggs and add them to the potatoes. Add the other ingredients.
3. With an adult's help, heat the oil in a frying pan.
4. Drop spoonfuls of the mixture into the oil. Flatten each pancake with a spoon.
5. Fry the pancakes on each side until they are brown and crispy.
6. Drain the pancakes on paper towels and serve them hot with applesauce or sour cream.

Playing Dreidel

Join in the fun of Hanukkah and play dreidel. The game began when the Jews were ruled by the Syrian Greeks. They were forbidden to read the Torah, their holy book, so they had to study it secretly. If they were caught, they quickly hid their books and began to play dreidel instead.

You will need:
• a dreidel (A dreidel is a spinning top with four sides. Each side is marked with a Hebrew letter. The letters stand for the words "Nes, Gadol, Hayah, Sham," which mean, "A great miracle happened here.")
• a pile of pennies (Each player starts with the same number of pennies.)

How to play:
1. Each player puts a penny in the middle.
2. Everyone takes turns spinning the dreidel. If it lands with this letter facing upwards:

נ (Nun), you do *N*othing

ג (Gimmel), you *G*rab everything in the middle

ה (Hey), you take *H*alf of the pennies

ש (Shin), you *S*hove another penny in

3. After each player's turn, everyone puts in another penny.
4. The winner is the person who gets all the pennies.

**If you enjoyed this book,
why not read *The Passover Story*?**

The famous story of Moses and how he helped the Jews escape from Egypt to the promised land is beautifully told in *The Passover Story*. The book also includes information about the significance of Passover and the Sedar meal today, a Passover recipe, and the words to a popular Passover song.